Historical Walks

from

The LEEDS & LIVERPOOL Canal

by John Dixon
with an historical introduction by Mike Clarke

Carnegie Publishing Ltd., 1990

The walks in this book were devised by John Dixon, the author of several excellent walking books covering areas in Lancashire and West Yorkshire. They were included in the recently published *The Leeds and Liverpool Canal: A History and Guide* by Mike Clarke, also by Carnegie Publishing, copies of which are available from good booksellers or direct from the publishers

---

Historic Walks from the Leeds and Liverpool Canal
by John Dixon

Copyright, © John Dixon, 1990
First published in this edition, July 1990

Published by Carnegie Publishing Ltd.,
18 Maynard Street, Preston PR2 2AL. Tel (0772) 881246

Printed by T. Snape & Co. Ltd., Boltons Court, Preston.

ISBN 0 948789 62 X

Historical introduction

THE Leeds and Liverpool Canal was the most successful long-distance canal in Britain. In 1906 it carried 2,337,401 tons of cargo an average distance of over twenty miles, producing around £180,000 in revenue. In overall terms of quantity of goods and distance carried, no other British canal could compare with this. The Birmingham Canal Navigation did carry more, at over seven million tons, but it did so only over short distances, the average being just eight miles. The Aire and Calder Navigation also carried slightly more, at 2.8 million tons, but here the larger size of the river locks meant that far larger boats could use the navigation.

One factor in the success of the Leeds and Liverpool was its sheer size. With a main line of 127¼ miles, it is the longest single canal in Britain. Just as important, the area through which it passes was – and is – one of the most heavily populated in the land. The canal linked

Liverpool, Wigan, Blackburn, Burnley, Skipton, Keighley, Shipley, Bingley, Bradford (via the Bradford Canal) and Leeds. These towns, and others in the area, were the cradle of the revolution in textile manufacture and the Leeds and Liverpool Canal, as probably the region's single most important transport facility, thus holds a particularly important place in English, and indeed world, history.

Unlike many canals, the Leeds and Liverpool was never tied to any one particular trade or traffic. Coal, wool, cotton, limestone, grain and general cargo were all carried in huge quantities by a wide range of carriers. Partly because of this and partly because of the sheer length of the canal, the Leeds and Liverpool boasted an immense diversity of traffic. Carriers developed for particular trades and several general services were operated so successfully for so long that in negotiations with the competing railway companies the canal company usually came out on top. For many years the canal beat off the railways' competition by being more competitive, more efficient and even, it was claimed, considerably quicker on some routes than the railways.

The initial impetus for the building of the Leeds and Liverpool came from east of the

Pennines, from landowners and merchants around Bradford who were anxious to increase the supply of limestone to their coal mines in the Bingley and Bradford area where it could be burnt to produce lime for land improvement and building purposes. They also wanted a cheap means of delivering coal to the limestone quarries in the Craven district to reduce the price of lime for the improvement of grazing lands in the area. Lastly, and very significantly, they felt that a canal would be a reliable and speedy through route for local textile products to the developing ports of Liverpool and Lancaster and the markets beyond.

For the Liverpool promoters there were very different reasons for wanting such a canal. They required a cheap and reliable supply of coal for their manufacturing and shipping businesses, together with the opportunity to tap the growing industries of Lancashire. It was this difference that was to lead to prolonged confrontation and almost to the collapse of the canal scheme.

Although we do not know the author, the *York Courant* of 7th August 1764 appears to have contained the first suggestion of a canal to link Lancashire and Yorkshire:

> As the Rivers Aire and Ribble may be so easily joined at different places and rendered

navigable between Leeds and Preston at an expense which gentlemen who have estates on the banks may readily supply it is thought proper to mention it to the public at this juncture.

Perhaps we can see here the hand of one John Stanhope, a prominent Bradford landowner and attorney who was to play a large part in the canal's promotion. Although he was primarily a lawyer, he was involved with various regulations governing the sale of woollen goods, and his brother, Walter, was a Leeds woollen merchant.

It seems to have been Stanhope who first engaged John Longbotham to survey a route. Longbotham started work in 1765. He wrote to Stanhope about his plan to link Preston with the River Aire, with two branches leading away from the canal at Walton, near Preston. One branch was to go north to Poulton, on the Wyre, for trade to Lancaster; the other was to the south, to Liverpool. Thus, at this early stage, Preston rather than Liverpool was to be the destination on the Lancashire side.

Eventually, after much disagreement and behind-the-scenes manoeuvres, an Act of Parliament was obtained for the building of a canal between the River Aire at Leeds and Liverpool, which missed the Wigan coalfield but which did

Walks from the Leeds & Liverpool Canal 7

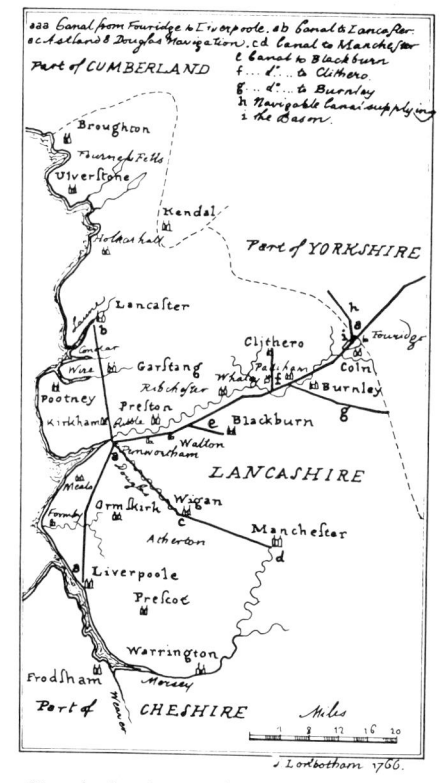

A copy of Longbotham's original survey of 1766, showing his first idea, for a canal to link the Ribble and Aire rivers.

allow for a junction with the Douglas Navigation so that boats could transfer to the river near Parbold in order to reach Wigan. This compromise was just enough for the Liverpool promoters of the canal to agree to the shorter but less attractive route through Lancashire.

On this basis, contruction of the canal began in 1770. Work began from both ends simultaneously. The Yorkshire end from Leeds to Gargrave involved some considerable engineering works and saw the building of several staircase locks, including the famous Bingley 5-rise and 3-rise. This section was completed and opened fairly quickly. Work on the Lancashire end also proceeded well at first and by 1774 the canal was opened as far as the junction with the Douglas Navigation.

And there the money ran out. Luckily, the two sections which were operational were viable in themselves. The trans-Pennine link was not completed until much later, in 1816, but both the Yorkshire and Lancashire ends were able to trade without being joined.

The overall aim, however, was to open the canal all the way from Leeds to Liverpool. When money became available, therefore, work began again. Since 1774 the towns of east Lancashire had grown very considerably with the rise of

Walks from the Leeds & Liverpool Canal

important new industries. When construction work did re-commence westwards from Gargrave, therefore, everyone was agreed that the route of the canal should be altered from that sanctioned by Parliament in 1770 so that it passed through the towns of Blackburn, Accrington, Burnley and Chorley, as well as Wigan, thus giving us the route which the canal follows today.

The long and successful commercial life of the canal is now at an end. Fortunately, the canal survived intact in the three decades or so since it ceased to be used for transport. Now, of course, its potential for leisure use is fully recognised; canalside warehouses have been renovated as tourist features in places like Wigan and Blackburn, and use of the canal by pleasure craft, fisherman — and walkers — is for ever on the increase.

Evidence of the canal's former use can be seen everywhere, however, and the observant walker can spot many different features of interest along the canal towpath.

Locks and bridges are the most obvious canal features, but look out for old deserted wharves and mooring points, for evidence of coke ovens in East Lancashire and limekilns in Yorkshire. Try to spot the ramps where horses would be

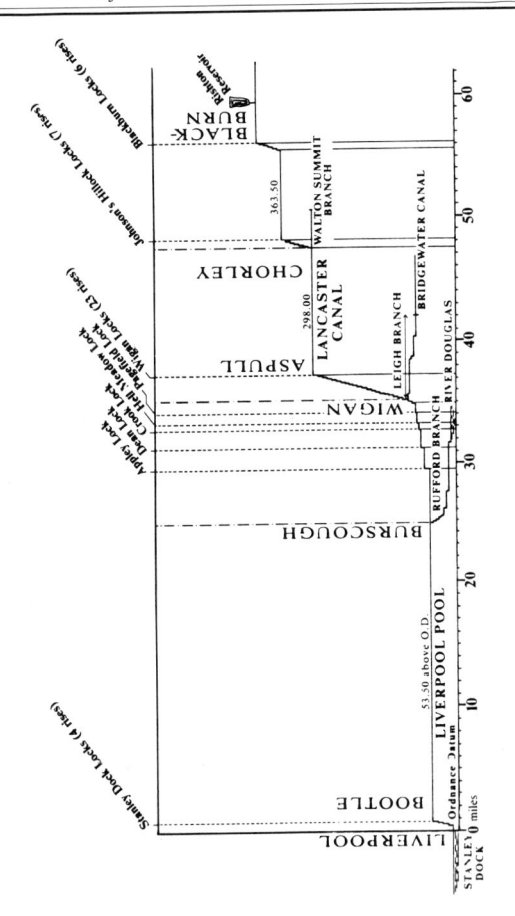

Walks from the Leeds & Liverpool Canal

(Schematic diagram of the Leeds & Liverpool Canal showing elevation profile and locations from Liverpool to Blackburn, including Bootle, Burscough, Wigan, Aspull, Chorley, and Blackburn, with branches to Stanley Dock, Rufford, Leigh (Bridgewater Canal), Lancaster Canal, Walton Summit Branch, and Rishton Reservoir. Locks shown: Stanley Dock Locks (4 rises), Appley Lock, Dean Lock, Crooke Lock, Wigan Locks (21 rises), Pagefield Lock, Ell Meadow Lock, Johnson's Hillock Locks (7 rises), Blackburn Locks (6 rises). Elevations: 53.50 above O.D. at Liverpool Pool, 298.00, 363.50.)

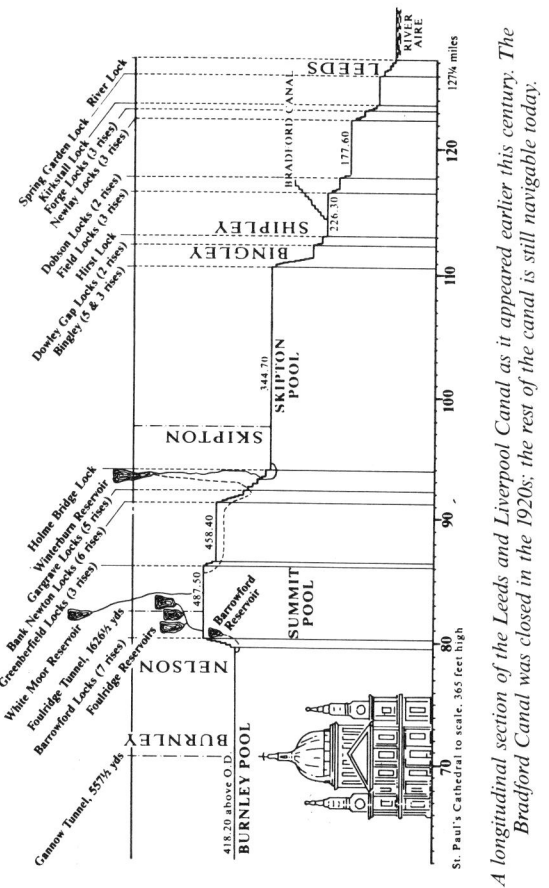

A longitudinal section of the Leeds and Liverpool Canal as it appeared earlier this century. The Bradford Canal was closed in the 1920s; the rest of the canal is still navigable today.

able to clamber out of the water if they had the misfortune to fall in. Where rollers are missing at bridges and tight bends, you can often see the grooves where towropes have cut away the stonework. And look out for old warehouses, canalside architecture and mills, as well as the very frequent evidence of old industrial development, so much of which owes its existence to the canal itself.

With careful observation, you should be able to appreciate the canal and its history more every time you walk along sections of it.

Walks from the Leeds & Liverpool Canal   13

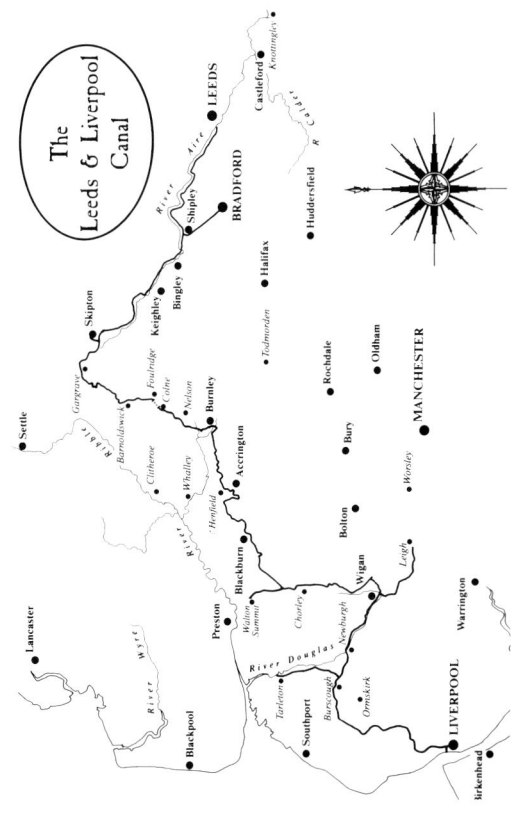

The Leeds and Liverpool Canal

Circular walks — introduction

THE aim of these walks is to give the walker the chance to explore some of the marvellous countryside and scenery through which the Leeds and Liverpool Canal passes. Many more walks could easily be devised, and the walker is invited to explore the rest of the canal and the areas around it using the thousands of public footpaths within easy reach of the towpath. The Ordnance Survey Pathfinder (1:25,000) maps are extremely useful for this kind of 'DIY' walking.

The maps in this book indicate the general route followed by the walks, but when it doubt, we recommend that walkers make use of the relevant O.S. maps. Please keep to the public footpaths and, where a particular route takes you past residential property, please try to respect the privacy of residents. Please also observe the Country Code. But, most of all, enjoy the walks.

Walk One

East Riddlesden — Rombalds Moor — Ilkley Moor — Addingham High Moor — Ghyll — West Riddlesden

Distance: 12 miles, circular. Allow 6 hours.
Grade: Moorland walking; good underfoot; wear walking boots.
Lunch: Packed lunch.
Evening Meal: Bridge Inn, Keighley Road.

TWELVE miles may seem rather a long walk but it is well worth the effort. The landscape we pass through on Yorkshire's most renouned moor is splendid, as are the views to be had from several points on the walk. We sample the historical delights of East Riddlesden Hall and walk through countryside heavily littered with Brigantian remains.

East Riddlesden Hall

East Riddlesden Hall is a typical large Yorkshire

house of the seventeenth century. The house was built for James Murgatroyd, a Halifax clothier, in around 1642, with a new range added in 1692.

The house is first viewed across a fish pond, part of a former grange of Bolton Priory that stood on the site before the Reformation. The visitor enters the house through a round-arched doorway flanked by fluted columns with a rose window above, all topped by battlements and pinnacles. This arrangement is repeated at the rear. Inside are collections of pewter, domestic period utensils and Yorkshire oak furniture.

To the left of the entrance is a row of servants' cottages dated 1642, and near the roadway are two seventeenth-century barns. The Great Barn is of around 1640 and houses a collection of farm carts and implements. The barn and the grounds can be viewed free; entry to the Hall costs £1.50. There is a gift shop and tea room.

East Riddlesden Hall to Brass Castle Stone Circle

Leave by the main gateway and cross the road to walk up to join the canal towpath at the swing bridge by the Marquis of Granby Inn. Follow the towpath to the right to leave via next bridge (No. 198). Walk up Swine Lane, around the corner then left to walk up Bury Lane track to Dean Hole Farm via gates. Follow the farm lane up to roadway, left, and walk up Street Lane to go right at crossroads. Walk up Ilkley Road, past Upwood Hall, to go

Walks from the Leeds & Liverpool Canal 17

over wall-stile on left at footpath sign. Walk on and over next stile. The stone circle is forty yards down on the right following the fence.

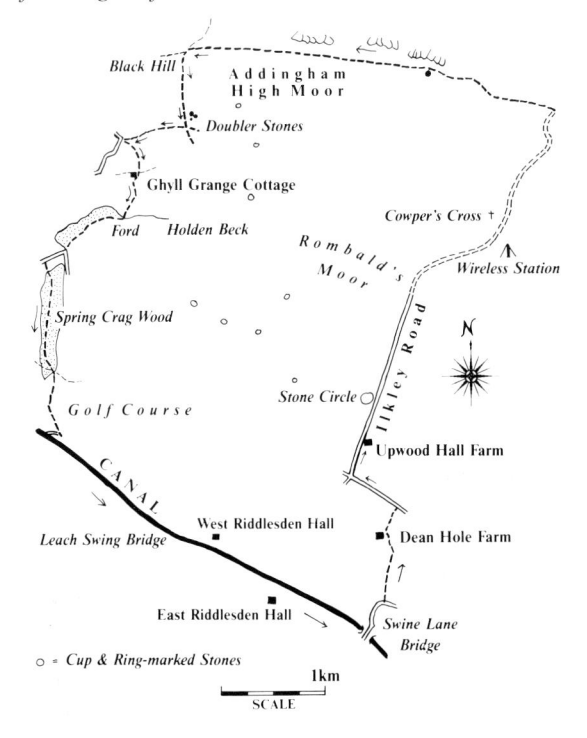

Brass Castle/Bradup Stone Circle

No finds are recorded from this badly damaged Bronze Age site. The circle, which measures some thirty feet across, contains twelve stones, less than half its original number.

On to Cowper's Cross

Return to the roadway and follow it on, past Bradup Farm, and on up (notice the well on the left dated 1853 T.H.X.S.) to go through gate below wireless station. Walk down the trackway to Cowper's Cross.

Standing in the centre of Rombalds Moor, Cowper's Cross gives one a fine vantage point above Ilkley and on over to the Yorkshire Dales. The cross has a date of 1883 with the initials ILB IM.

Follow the track on down to the tarmack surface, then follow the left-hand track to Silver Well Cottage. Follow path on to go through wall-gate by shed and on through the ferns to join lower pathway. Follow the path on to the railed-off 'Swastika Stone' at the top of Woodhouse Crag.

The Swastika Stone

Rombalds Moor was an important area of settle-

ment throughout the
Bronze Age and into
the Iron Age. Before the
coming of the Romans
an important Celtic
political and religious
centre was established
at Ilkley.

It was during these later Brigantian times that the 'Swastika Stone' was carved. It represents the major river valleys in this mid-Pennine area and the major tribal centres. The NW arm shows the Craven Aire Gap and the important settlement at Gargrave Caput; the NE arm is the Upper Wharfe Valley and Grassington settlement; the SW arm is the Lower Aire Valley and the 'caput' of Leeds; the SE arm is the Lower Wharfe Valley leading over to Tadcaster and York; the loop represents the Brigantian capital at Aldborough.

Roman dominance was to break up the political confederacy of the Briganties by establishing forts and towns upon the tribal centres. However, the 'Swastika Stone' still remains mapping out those early Celtic realms that were to rise again after the fall of Rome.

Follow the cragside path on, over wall-stile and on over Addingham Moor to go over two wall-stiles (notice the boundary stone to the side of this last stile I/M – Ilkley/Morton, ILB 1893). Follow the path on to go over five stiles and on to a cairn-marked crossroads in paths of Black Hill. Take the left-hand path and walk on to go over wall-

stile. Follow the path directly on down the moor to go through fence-gate below the wind eroded rocks of Doubler Stones.

Doubler Stones

The mushroom-shaped, wind-eroded rocks of Doubler Stones conjure up much in the imagination, especially when the 'cup and ring' marks are examined on their upper surfaces. There are over 250 examples of this Bronze Age carving within the few square miles of Rombalds Moor. Upon our walk thus far we have passed about thirty of the stones (use the O.S. Pathfinder map to locate them). The carvings are varied and include cups, many concentrically ringed, ladder markings and swastikas. The stones differ in size and a number are difficult to find, especially when the bracken growth is high.

Back to East Riddlesden Hall

Walk on to the farm lane and follow it on to the right, through gateway and down to next gate. Turn around and now follow right-hand wall on to go through gateway and on down the track to driveway. Walk down the driveway to go through small gate on left opposite Ghyll Grange cottage. Walk around the building and on to go through gates on right. Follow track down to go through gateway. Walk down the field to go over foot-bridge under pipeline.

Follow path to the right to go through gateway and on following left-hand fence to go over fence-stile into wood. Walk down, across the brook and up and on, following edge of wood, to go down bridleway and to go over stile by gate onto roadway. Walk down the road to go through gate on left at footpath sign. Follow right-hand wall to enter wood via stile. Follow path into wood and after a short way take the left hand fork on up and continue on to leave wood by wall-stile up on left. Follow right-hand path down to go over stile by gate onto golf course. Follow right-hand wall on, then 'yellow staked' pathway down to join gravel trackway and on down, past the club house to go down the trackway on right and onto the canal tow-path. Follow the towpath on to the swingbridge at the Marquis of Granby Inn. Walk down the road to East Riddlesden Hall car park.

Walk Two

Skipton — Flasby — Gargrave — Skipton

Distance: 10 miles, circular. 11 miles with Kirk Sink Roman Villa. Allow 2½ hours from Skipton to Gargrave plus time to explore the Roman villa and Gargrave village; 2½ hours back along the canal. All at an easy pace.

Grade: Easy, but wear walking boots. Do not go up on the fell if the mist is down.

Lunch: Masons Arms, Gargrave.

Evening Meal: Royal Shepherd, Skipton.

IN this easy walk we take in the rugged splendour of the highlands above the market town of Skipton. To the north east rises Rylstone Fell and Embsay Moor, a great wilderness from whence the stones were hewn to build the castle and town of Skipton. To the north west, our route is marked by the pike of Sharp Haw, sentinal to the upper Aire Valley, from which vantage point the lay of Craven is overviewed. We descend quickly from the rough gritstones of Flasby Fell to the locks east of Gargrave to return by way of the towpath to Skipton town.

Skipton Parish Church to Flasby

Walk down by the church and over the bridge to turn right and walk up Chapel Hill, left at the fork and on up to go over wall-stile by gateway. Walk up the hill to go over wall-stile by gate. The Battery earthwork is over on the left. Walk on down the hill to go over stiles and up onto bypass. Cross the road and go over fence-stile opposite. Cross the field to go over fence-stile. Walk directly over the golf course to go over corner stile in section of walling. Follow the wall around to go through stone gap-stile and follow wall on to go over stile by gate. Follow left-hand fence over on the left, down to go over stile onto Brackenley Lane, left and walk up the road to the road junction. Cross the road and pass over stile opposite. Walk on directly to go over fence-stile near electricity pole. Follow left-hand hedgerow, then fence on, to go over stile by gate onto road. Follow road on, around two corners and on to go through gateway on left at third corner. Follow trackway on through two gates onto moor. Leave the trackway and walk up on to the moor and follow guide-posts to go through gateway. (To the left are the Craggs and the Iron Age enclosure; in front rises the pike of Sharp Haw and on the right, Rough Haw. Far over on the right Rylston Fell dominates with Norton Tower at its peak.) Our path now goes between Sharp Haw and Rough Haw, so follow the staked pathway on in the direction of Sharp Haw to veer sharply off the path to the right before path ascends to summit. Walk on to (in summer this meadow is covered in flax) go through field-gate in wall. Walk across the ling on a right-diagonal down to go over wall-stile by small gate. Walk on on a left-diagonal and follow the path down and over to the right of the clough and on to go through field-gate in wall. Walk down the field to far left-hand corner to join trackway via gate. Follow trackway down into Flasby.

Flasby to Gargrave Church

Turn left at the wall post-box and walk down the lane to go over a fence-stile on the right at footpath sign. Walk up to go over next stile. Walk on on a left-diagonal to go over fence-stile (the ruin of Flasby Hall is over on the left and the folly tower down on the left). Follow left-hand fence on down to follow yellow marker-posts on to go up and through kissing-gate onto road. Left, and walk down the road, over the bridge (Eshton Hall is over on the right) and on to road junction. Go over wall-stile on the left and cross the field on a right-diagonal to go over stile by gate. Follow fence to the right to go over fence-stile (a magnificent view of Flasby Hall is to be had from here). Walk up the field veering slightly to the left, then directly on along the brow of the hill to go over stile by pine plantation on the left. Walk down to go over next stile. Cross the field, veering left, to go over stile then footbridge and up onto the canal. Follow the path down to the locks and cross the footbridge onto the canal towpath. Walk up the tow path to leave via the second bridge. Follow gated

Walks from the Leeds & Liverpool Canal 25

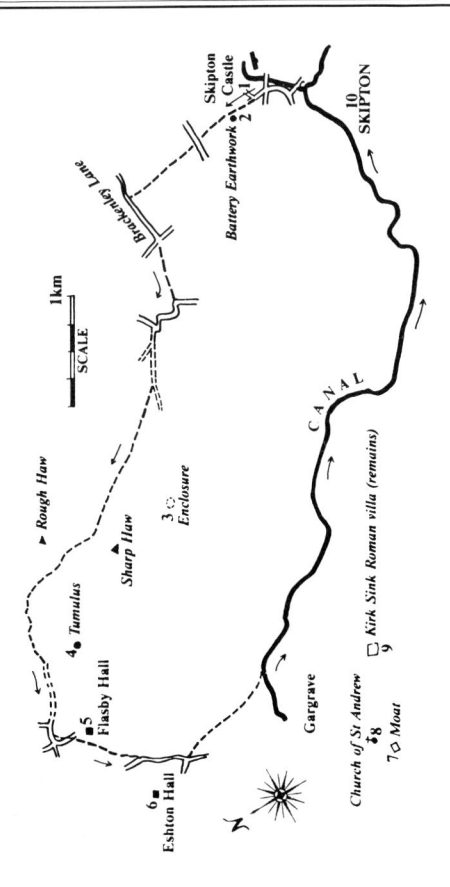

pathway on to the Swan Inn and on to go over the bridge to the Masons Arms and the parish church.

St. Andrew's Church to Roman Villa site

Walk down the lane by the side of the church and on into farmyard. (Here ask the farmer for permission to walk upon the site and section of Roman road). Follow the footpath on to Kirk Sink earthworks.

Gargrave to Skipton

Make your way back to the canal towpath and follow it on down into the centre of Skipton (notice the swing bridges on the way).

Points of interest

1. As we walk up High Street, where the market is held, the Church of Holy Trinity is up on the left, with the round towers of the Castle entrance over on the right. The church dates back to some time before 1120, but the earliest remains today are Decorated in style and date from around 1350. The rest is mainly Perpendicular, with seventeenth-century restorations. The figures on the First Earl of Cumberland, Henry Clifford, are worth viewing, dating from about 1542. A good

guide book enables one to explore the church in full.
2. The Battery is a square earthwork on the summit of Park Hill. Some suggest that it is a Civil War Parliamentary gun emplacement used during the siege of 1642. Others see it as a Roman signal station above the Aire Gap.
3. The enclosure near Sharp Haw is an Iron Age hill-top site, probably a redoubt for the capital manor of the Celtic 'cantrev' of Craven, being at that time sited at Gargrave.
4. A Bronze Age tumulus and cairn have been identified here on Flasby Fell. Also, a Bronze Age rapier was found in the clough coming down from the fell – now on display in the Craven Museum, Skipton.
5. The village of Flasby is mentioned in the Domesday Book. The central farmhouse is a seventeenth-century building; Flasby Hall is wholly Victorian. Some years ago, in the grounds of the Hall, the remains of an ancient chapel were discovered, its origins unknown.
6. Eshton Hall, now a retirement home, was built in around 1826 by the architect George Webster of Kendal for Sir Mathew Wilson, and what a splendid frontage it presents.
7. The moated manor house site to the west of the church is locally known as the Garris, once the home of the Gargraves of Gargrave, having their seat here since the twelfth century. Gargrave was a 'double' manor – on both sides of the river. The

northern moated manor house site of the de Longevilers is sited above North Street.
8. The church of St. Andrew was established in Anglo-Danish times and a number of ancient cross fragments from the tenth century can be viewed inside the church. The building itself was mostly rebuilt in 1852, while the tower dates from 1521. Across the way is the Masons Arms, an excellent lunch stop – good service, good ale, all at very reasonable prices.
9. Kirk Sink Roman Villa, built upon an Iron Age site, consists of a second-century villa and bath house, two third/fourth-century houses and an administration block, all within a walled and ditched courtyard. Just outside the complex is a very good cambered section of Roman road.
10. The town of Skipton owes much to the nineteenth century, but its incremental layout and development owes more to the medieval, leaving the visitor many varied changes in streetscape to observe and enjoy. The main focus for the town is the castle of the Cliffords, first built in Norman times and added to over the centuries. The outer bailey gateway, with rotund semicircular projections, leads us into one of the finest castles to be found in the North of England. A good historical guide to the church and castle is available in the church.

Walk Three

East Marton — Bank Newton — Ingthorpe Grange — East Marton

Distance: 5 miles circular.
Grade: Easy walking, but wear light boots or stout shoes.
Lunch/Evening Meal: Cross Keys Inn, East Marton or Abbots Harbour (lunch and cream teas from 8 a.m. to 6 p.m. each day), East Marton.

FOR many who walk the nearby Pennine Way the three Domesday manors of Marton, Newton and Ingthorpe are passed by in the push for Gargrave. The folly of others – for not tarrying awhile – is our gain. Here, amid the rolling hillsides of Craven, we shall discover Jacobean farmsteads and monastic granges still unknown to the crowds in this splendid rural backwater.

East Marton to Bank Newton Locks

Your car can be parked on the side road by the telephone box or on the far rear Cross Keys car park

Walks from the Leeds & Liverpool Canal

as long as you check with the landlord that this is acceptable.

Walk down the lane to the rear of the pub to Abbots Harbor and Sawley House, then over bridge no. 162 onto the towpath. Walk under the bridge and follow the delightfully tree-shaded towpath on through its many curves to leave via a gate above Newton Grange. Follow canalside lane on and over bridge no. 165 to pass over stile on left onto the towpath. Walk on and take in the six locks at Bank Newton.

Bank Newton Locks to Newton Hall

After viewing the locks return to bridge no. 165 and back over the stile to walk down the lane, passing Cald Newton Farm, to the road junction. The imposing gable of Newton Hall is now in front of you.

Newton Hall to Ingthorpe Grange

Turn left at the junction and follow the road past the quaint wayside farmstead to go through a field-gate on the left. Follow the stream up for a short way then walk on across the field to go over wall-stile onto roadway. Follow the road on around the bend and on to go over wall-stile on left opposite hawthorne bush. Walk up the hill on your right to go through wall-gate at summit. Walk over the brow of the hill on a left diagonal and on down to go through field-gate. Walk on over the hill, bearing right and on down to go over stile by gateway over on the left. Walk over the rise on a left diagonal and on down to go over fence-stile, brook and wall-stile. Pass through the gateway over on the right and cross the field on a left diagonal to go through green wall-gate at Ingthorpe Grange barn. Left, and follow lane on to view the spectacular frontage of Ingthorpe Grange.

Ingthorpe Grange to East Marton Church

Follow Ingthorpe Lane on to the roadway at East Marton, noticing on the way the splendid views of Flasby and Rylstone fells to the north-east. Left, then cross the road to walk down the lane to the church.

Church of St. Peter to Cross Keys Inn

After visiting the church leave via stile at the top right-hand corner of the churchyard to walk directly on (notice double-arched canal bridge down to the right) to the Cross Keys Inn, via wall-stile.

Points of interest

1. Mullioned frontage cottage with a dated doorhead 1698 and the initials A.A.A.
2. Abbots Harbor and Sawley House; the latter is said to incorporate within its fabric the remains of a monks' rest house established in the twelfth century by the convent at Sawley. Notice the two Early English windows with the cross above.
3. Opposite the TV mast set on the edge of the towpath is an iron milestone: Leeds 37¼ miles, Liverpool 90 miles.
4. The six locks at Bank Newton and the old lock-keeper's cottage. A further six locks are to be

Walks from the Leeds & Liverpool Canal

encountered on the way down to Gargrave.

5. A delightful seventeenth-century farmhouse at Cald Newton, surrounded by a walled garden that is a profusion of colour in the summer months.
6. Newton Hall, a seventeenth-century yeoman farmhouse, once home to the Banks and Townley families. Adjoining the Hall is a small chantry chapel, now an outhouse in the garden. The aisled barn is worthy of note.
7. Ingthorpe Grange, an imposing seventeenth-century house with a chapel at the rear. Above the first-floor window of the porch is a triangular panel informing us that '**** Baldwin birth was 1671'; below the window is the datestone of the house, H.B.B. 1672. Ingthorpe was a bercary (sheep farm) established by Bolton Priory in around 1301. Before 1295 it was farmed for wheat by four ploughmen.
8. St. Peter's, East Marton. Short, broad Norman tower, but the nave, chancel and south aisle are nineteenth-century in date. Inside is a frag-ment of a late Anglo-Norse cross of Viking style depicting the god Thor with his hammer, defending himself against the earth serpent. South of the church are the earthwork remains of the c.1445 Hall of the Martons, lords of the manor, and the ancient fish ponds.
9. The double-arched canal bridge came about when the level of the roadway had to be raised. This spot is a haven for anglers from the Craven

district.
10. The Cross Keys Inn offers a good variety of food and a fine selection of ales within 'olde worlde' surroundings – plenty of bar space, good place settings with traditional furniture and two large open fires, all add up to a cosy evening atmosphere. The day I was there I had 'fisherman's pie with veg' at £2.85 – served within five minutes – and it was very good and filling.
11. Abbots Harbor serves home-made traditional farmhouse food amid a tranquil setting. The village biscuits in particular are a must – delicious. Abbots can also accommodate two adults and two children bed and breakfast, by appointment – Tel: Earby 843207. Good food here too, and more varied than the Cross Keys which is a Chef and Brewer house.

Walk Four

Salterforth — Barnoldswick — Thornton — Earby — Kelbrook — Salterforth

Distance: 8 miles, circular. If you wish to shorten the walk, buses run every half hour between Earby and Salterforth. Allow 5 hours, including visits and lunch hour.
Grade: Easy walking, but wear light boots.
Lunch: The Red Lion, Earby.
Evening Meal: Anchor Inn, Salterforth.
Start: Anchor Inn, Salterforth, by canal bridge no. 151, but the walk can just as easily be started from Barnoldswick, Earby or Kelbrook.

THIS ramble takes us through five West Craven settlements that have their origins in the seventh century, before Craven was a Celtic kingdom in itself. Since then Angles, Scandinavians and Lancastrians, have made inroads in this land of drumlins between the southern gritstone of the Pennines and the northern limestone of the Dales. The hilly

36 Walks from the Leeds & Liverpool Canal

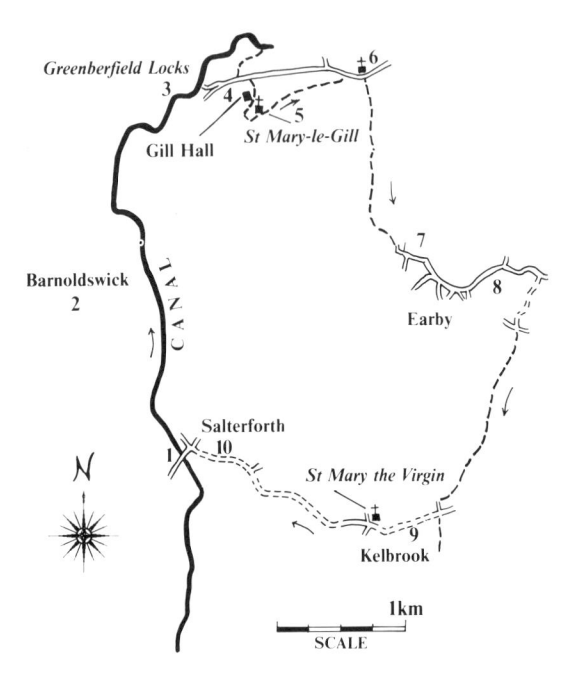

landscape of West Craven was caused by retreating glaciers depositing boulder clay over nodules on the limestone floor. With churches secreted away from the main settlements one could well believe that we are within that realm attributed to Thomas Hardy. All in all, a delightful arcadia of rural tranquility to discover at our leisure.

Anchor Inn to St. Mary-le-Gill

Follow the towpath northwards, passing Barnoldswick Marina and on past the Silentnight and Rolls Royce factories to the rural setting of the three Greenberfield Locks. After the locks the towpath changes to the opposite bank of the canal via a footbridge. From this point we follow the waymarked Pendle Way through Gill, Thornton and Earby to just above the village of Kelbrook. Even given the waymarking, the route will still be described.

After crossing the footbridge, follow the curve of the canal to the right and after it curves to the left pass over the wall-stile on your left. Follow the path up to follow the Rolls Royce factory fence over to the right to go over the stile by gate. Follow path to the left to go over wall-stile by gate onto lane. You are now standing on the line of the Roman road between Ribchester and Elslack. Cross the main road and walk down the grass verge to go through a small gate opposite factory entrance. Follow path up, passing Gill Hall, to enter churchyard via gated stile.

St. Mary-le-Gill to Thornton Church

Follow the path on the outside of the south churchyard wall down to go over Gill Syke up onto the golf course.

Cross the course directly to go through kissing-gate after gap in conifers. (As we leave the golf course the tower of Thornton Church comes into view along with the southern Dales, Pen-y-Ghent, Bowland Fells, Pendle and the summit of Weets above Barlic. To the right of the church tower can be seen the start of the wild Pennine 'Bronte' Moors). Walk directly across the brow of the hill to go over fence-stile, and on to go over hedge-stile onto roadway. Cross the road and walk on to Thornton Church.

On to Earby Mines Museum

Pass over the stile opposite the church porch and walk across the field (notice the field-well on the left) to go through kissing-gate and on to go through wall-stile. Cross the field directly to gate at bend in road. With your back to the road cross the field on a left diagonal to go through stone-gap stile in fence. Cross the field to go over stile by gate, then walk directly on to go through stone stile. Cross the field in front of The Grange on a left diagonal to go through stile by gate. Walk down the field on a right diagonal to go over fence stile, and on to go over wall-stile into lane behind All Saints Church. Walk down to the roadway and across into School Lane, then along and down to Earby Mines Museum on the left.

Earby Mines Museum to Red Lion Inn

Walk along the road, passing Wardle Storeys mill, and

on into Water Street to enter Old Earby. Walk on along the road to the Red Lion Inn.

Red Lion to Kelbrook Church

Continue along the road, past the Youth Hostel on Birch Hall Lane and on up to go through stile by gate set back on the right. Follow right-hand wall on to go over wall-stile, and on following right hand fence/hedge to go through stone stile into old Mill Lane. Walk on to the roadway, turn left and walk up to go through stile on right. Walk on to go through gateway, and on following trackway to go over wall-stile. Cross the field directly and follow Moor Hall farm track up to go through stile by gate. Walk on, across the stream and on to follow right-hand fence to go through field-gate. Follow old track on to go over stile by gate. Cross the field directly to go through gateway. Walk on, veering right, to enter old lane via stile. Walk on to the junction. (The eighteenth-century Tunsted Farm is just on a way, over the stile on the right.) Turn left and walk on to Heads Lane. Here we leave the Pendle Way to follow the lane down to the top of Kelbrook. Follow the riverside trackway on to the church of St. Mary the Virgin.

On to Anchor Inn, Salterforth

Walk across the bridge and on to the Craven Heifer. Walk up the track on the right of the inn and follow it on to go over a stile. Follow right-hand hedgerow on to go over stile at wall. Down the steps to cross the line of the old railway and on to go over stile. Follow left-hand fence for a short way to go over stile on left. Walk down to go over footbridge (two large stones set on piers). Walk on to go through gateway and on, following hedgerow, to go through gate. Follow track on, over stile, to follow goit on, over stiles to Salterforth. Cross the road and walk up by the bus stop to the Anchor Inn.

Points of interest

1. The Anchor Inn. Stalactites have formed in the cellar by water seeping through the limestone.
2. Barnoldswick's social and economic development can be traced through its architecture. It well deserves its title of 'Lancashire's best kept secret'. Good and varied shopping, good pubs, clean and tidy streets and very friendly folk, as one would expect from 'old Yorkshire'.
3. Greenberfield Locks, within a rustic setting second to none.
4. Gill Hall is a late-sixteenth-century building built by the Banisters, the first grantees of the Manor of Barnoldswick after the Dissolution. As can be seen from the east gable, the house was once much larger.
5. The Cistercian monks from Fountains Abbey first came to Barnoldswick in 1147 to establish a convent here. But at that time, during the reign of

King Stephen, the house suffered from robbers, poor land and a bleak site, and in five years the monks had moved to their new site at Kirkstall. The main fabric dates from the rebuilding of 1524, though the roof and lancet east window belong to the thirteenth century. The interior is laid out with Jacobean box-pews and a complete three-decker pulpit with octagonal sounding board. A leaf-shaped sword of the Late Bronze Age was discovered near the church on Swilber Hill.
6. St. Mary's, Thornton. The tower is Perpendicular and contains several carved stones within its fabric. In the churchyard stands an octagonal well-house of 1764.
7. Earby Mines Museum is housed within the old grammar school of 1658, itself sited upon the foundations of a Cluniac Priory of c.1145. The museum contains over 600 lead mining relics from the Yorkshire Dales and other mining areas, plus a reconstructed crusher and many working models of mining operations. Open from the last Sunday in March to the last Sunday in October and Saturdays June to September. Opening times: Sundays 2 p.m. – 6 p.m; Thursdays 2 p.m. – 9 p.m; Saturdays 2 p.m. – 6 p.m. Small admission charge.
8. The Red Lion Inn is a typical working village pub serving good meals and good ale in very good company.
9. Kelbrook, along with Earby, Thornton and

Barnoldswick, is mentioned in the Domesday Survey, but the village reflects more of the eighteenth and mid-nineteenth centuries. A noisy little river flows through the centre of the village, giving it a romantic air.

10. Sited upon an ancient salt way, Salterforth is a seventeenth- and eighteenth-century hamlet. In Domesday it is referred to as 'the other Earby' and even today Old Earby and Salterforth have much in common.

Walks from the Leeds & Liverpool Canal

Walk Five

Foulridge — Blacko — Barrowford — Foulridge

Distance: 8 miles, or two walks of 4 miles each, using the southern end of Foulridge Tunnel as the mid-point in the 'figure-eight'. Allow 4 hours, excluding lunch and Heritage Centre visit.
Grade: Easy, but wear light boots.
Lunch: Cross Gaits Inn, Blacko.
Evening Meal: New Inn, Foulridge/White Bear, Barrowford.
Start: The walk begins from Foulridge Wharf, but you may choose to start at Park Hill Heritage Centre at Barrowford. Both have parking facilities.

AN opportunity here to explore the highest section of the canal, as well as gaining a glimpse of Pendle. The route follows sections of the Pendle Way, but we stray off to visit gems that the route planners have missed. A walk that you will want to return to many times.

44   *Walks from the Leeds & Liverpool Canal*

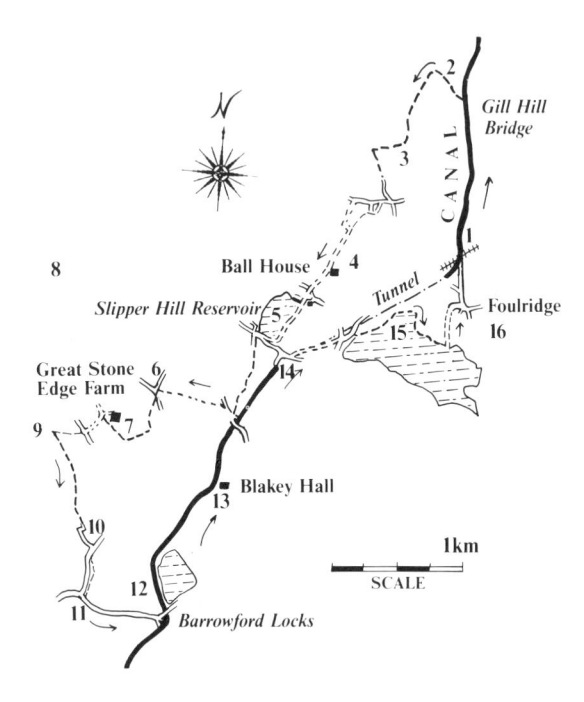

Foulridge Wharf to Slipper Hill Reservoir

Follow the towpath northwards to Mill Hill Bridge No. 149 (milestone Leeds 44¼ miles, Liverpool 83 miles). Walk over the bridge to go through right-hand gateway, then follow trackway on to go over stile by gate into Country Brook Mill yard (listen to the clatter of those Lancashire looms). Walk up the yard and on up the leafy lane (notice mill lodge on right) into the tiny hamlet of Hey Fold. Continue on to Mount Pleasant Chapel. Pass over a stile on the left just before the Chapel and cross the field to follow the track to the road junction at Hill Top. Turn right and walk up the road for a short way to go through waymarked gated wall-stile on left. Cross the field on a right diagonal to go over fence-stile. Walk a few yards down into the farmyard to go over stile on right and cross the driveway to go over next stile. Follow wall around to the left and on to go through wall-stile. Walk down the old lane, passing the rear of Ball House (we will be viewing the front of the building later), to pass over a stile at the bottom. Walk on to enter tree-lined pathway via wall-stile, and on to Slipper Hill Reservoir.

If you wish to return now to Foulridge, then follow the reservoir path to leave by waymarked stile at corner and walk down to the southern entry to Foulridge Tunnel. Follow directions to Foulridge Wharf and New Inn.

Ridge Wharf

For the longer walk follow the path around the reservoir to leave by white gate. Cross the road and walk over the bridge to go over stile on right, walk on to go over next stile and on to go over stile by gate. Follow house fence on, then hedgerow, over stile and on, through gateway to follow right-hand hedge on to go through old wall-stile. Cross the field veering left to go through stile by gate. Follow wall down to Lower Wanless farmyard gate. Pass through gap in hedge up on the right and walk across the farm lane to go over footbridge. Follow the ancient trackway up, via stiles, to the Cross Gaits Inn where a surprising offer awaits you!

On to Park Hill Heritage Centre

Come out of the pub and walk across to a house dated J.H. 1860 to go over stile at side of house. Cross the field to go through stile by far left-hand gateway and on to go over wall-stile, then down to go over fence-stile (before this stile a path on the left leads to the front of Lower Stone Edge Farm if you wish to view). Follow the fence up to go over corner stile and walk directly on to go over stile by gate (Great Stone Edge and Blacko Tower now come into view, while over on the left the great Lion of Pendle rises above Stang Top). Walk on, over stile by gate, and on to go over next stile. Turn left and pass over stile, then follow wall down to roadway via stiles. Pass over stile by gate opposite and walk down the field on a right diagonal to go over fence-stile. Follow path through the wood and over stiles onto Water-meetings Farm Lane. Cross the bridge then turn immediately left into pathway. Follow the riverside path down, via gates and stiles, into Higherford to go over the old pack-horse bridge on the left. Follow the cobbled lane on to cross the roadway. Walk down, past the Old Bridge Inn, to go through stile by bridge. Follow path on into the Heritage Centre car park.

Heritage Centre to Foulridge Tunnel

Follow the road up from the Heritage Centre on the right-hand footpath to go over stile by gate near motorway. Follow trackway down to go over bridge No. 143 onto towpath. Follow the towpath up Barrowford Locks, passing the ancient Blakey Hall over on the right just before the bridge, to the entrance of Foulridge Tunnel.

From here you can return to Barrowford by walking above the tunnel, over the bridge and on to the roadway. Left, and walk up to the entrance of Slipper Hill Reservoir. Follow earlier directions.

To Foulridge Wharf/New Inn

Walk above tunnel, over the bridge and on to the roadway. Right, over line of old railway, then left to walk along a trackway to roadway. Cross the road and walk up onto Lake Burwain Marine (Look across at the hillside for a view of Ball House). Follow the path around the lake to leave by waymarked lane on left. Walk up to cross the road and walk down next track into Sycamore Rise Road. Walk directly on to enter trackway on the right at Ivy Cottage. Follow it on down to the road. The New Inn is up to the left across the main road. The Wharf is directly down to the left.

Points of interest

1. Foulridge Wharf and warehouse were built in 1815. Raw American cotton was brought up from Liverpool to supply the local mills. Today converted barges run canal trips from here. In 1912 a cow fell into the canal at the Barrowford end of the tunnel and swam the distance to Foulridge. A photo of the swimming cow can be seen in the Hole in the Wall pub nearby.
2. Country Brook Mill stands on the boundary of Lancashire and the old West Riding of Yorkshire. A number of old Lancashire looms still weave cloth here today.
3. Hey Fold is an early-eighteenth-century hamlet, at that time the home of Mary Barrit, the first woman evangelist in the area. Mount Pleasant Chapel was originally two cottages, converted by the Rev. John Barrit in 1822.
4. Slipper Hill Reservoir is one of six feeder reservoirs used to top up the canal at this, its highest point. The house across the water was once used as a shooting and fishing lodge by the directors of the canal company.
5. Ball House was built by the Quaker, 'Blind' John Moore, in 1627 and is possibly the smallest gentry house in the Lancashire Pennines.
6. 'Good ale tomorrow for nothing', an offer that has been open to all since 1736 at the Cross Gaits Inn. A highly recommended lunch stop.

Walks from the Leeds & Liverpool Canal

7. Great and Lower Stone Edge are two farmsteads displaying much of their seventeenth-century origins.
8. Blacko Tower, built in around 1890 by Jonathan Stansfield to obtain a view over Ribblesdale. A much-loved landmark.
9. Here, where Pendle Water meets Blacko Water, stands the whitewashed seventeenth-century farmstead of Watermeetings, built by the Hargreaves family, who were among the principal tenants after the deforestation of 1507. The spur of land above where the waters meet is the haunt of local modern witches ('white' witches, so I am informed) who ply their craft and frolic naked in the nocturnal hours at the time of their pagan festivals.
10. Higherford's buildings owe much to the seventeenth and eighteenth centuries. The 'Owd Brig' is a packhorse bridge built between 1583 and 1591 on the old Gisburn to Colne road. From the apex of this bridge, John Wesley preached to the folk of Barrowford in the 1770s.
11. Park Hill, Pendle Heritage Centre, contains exhibitions on local farming and weaving, local history and architecture, and a video story of the Pendle Witches. Outside is a walled eighteenth-century herb garden and the frame of an early-sixteenth-century cruck barn. Opening times: Easter to last Sunday in November – Tuesday, Wednesday, Thursday, Saturday, Sunday and Bank Holiday Mondays, 2.00 p.m. to 4.30 p.m.

Admission charge. The Heritage Centre has produced a book *A Walk through Barrowford* that allows you to explore this delightful village in full, a good buy at £2.00.

12. Barrowford Locks and lock-keeper's cottage.
13. Blakey Hall, rebuilt in the eighteenth century, re-using many late-sixteenth-century features of the original house of Simon Blakey (c.1690), a devout Catholic who suffered heavy fines for his recusancy.
14. Foulridge Tunnel, 1,640 yards long. Barges were 'legged' through the tunnel – men lay on planks fixed to the boat and 'walked' along the tunnel walls. The horses were walked along a path above the tunnel.
15. Foulridge Reservoir, now renamed Lake Burwain, was constructed in 1793 to supply the summit level of the canal. It is now also used for leisure purposes – boating, fishing and walking and contains within its environs a great variety of wildlife, including the great-crested grebe.
16. Foulridge is centred around a village green surrounded by old weavers' cottages. The New Inn makes for a good lunch or evening meal stop – the pub even has a resident ghost; the landlord will tell you all about it over a pint of good ale. Across from the pub stands the seventeenth-century Breeze House, built by John Holgate, and records show that bull-baiting took place here at one time.

Walk Six

Weavers' Triangle, Burnley — Brierfield — Queen's Mill — Towneley Hall — Burnley

Distance: 10 miles circular; allow six hours with lunch at Harle Syke.
Grade: Easy walking, but wear light boots.
Lunch: The Craven Heifer or the Commercial, Harle Syke.

WITH the industrial revolution and the building of the Leeds and Liverpool Canal, Burnley grew to become the world's leading cotton cloth producer. Though 'King Cotton' has all but gone, the legacy of that age lingers on to intrigue those who have a fascination for a wealth of historical, cultural and industrial heritage that has gone into the making of this town on the banks of the River Brun.

The Weavers' Triangle

Within the 'Triangle' are to be found former spinning mills and weaving sheds, engine and loom

52   Walks from the Leeds & Liverpool Canal

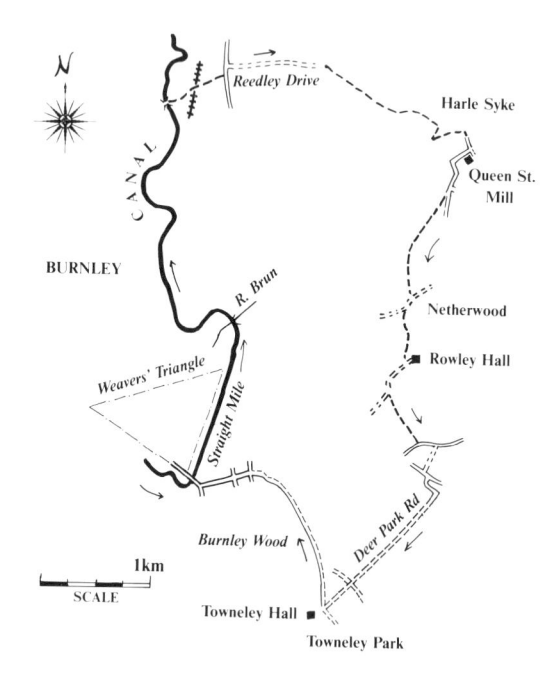

foundries, canalside warehouses and the homes of the former weavers. The Weavers' Triangle Visitor Centre, on Manchester Road, is housed in the former wharfmaster's house and canal toll office. Displayed inside are all aspects of Burnley's former industrial age, and with the restored canal wharf it provides an

Walks from the Leeds & Liverpool Canal

interesting setting. The centre is open to the public free of charge, on several afternoons each week during the summer months and on most bank holidays. Tel: (0282) 30055.

Visitor Centre to Queen Street Mill Museum

Go through the white gate opposite the Visitor Centre and follow the towpath on, passing British Waterways dock then above the town along the 'Straight Mile' (notice Pendle Hill over on the left and the Cliviger Gorge over on the right) to pass by the side of Thompson Park (once part of the Bank Hall Estate) and over the River Brun. The towpath now winds its way into the Forest of Pendle and we leave the path by way of the field access bridge after road bridge No. 134. Follow the path on to go over the railway bridge then cross the football fields to the top left-hand corner to go through iron gate and on to the road. Cross the road and walk up Reedly Drive, over on the left, to the very top. You come out on a new estate over on right. Cross the road and go through the Victorian gateway opposite and follow track on and round to the main roadway. Turn left and cross the road to footpath sign. Follow the pathway on past the rear of the houses to go over fence-stile. Walk on to follow right-hand wall on, through wall-stile and on to go through next wall-stile. Follow footpath on by side of houses to go over stile and on down the trackway, right and down through the farmyard onto the roadway. Turn left and walk along the road, past the Craven Heifer and The Commercial, past the post office to turn right into Queen Street. Walk down to the Mill Museum.

Queen Street Mill

This is the only surviving steam-powered cotton mill in Britain, built in 1894 at the height of the cotton industry. The working mill gives one an insight into the conditions of Victorian factory life. During viewing hours the magnificent steam engine, 'Peace', powers over 300 deafening Lancashire looms in the imposing weaving shed. Cotton cloth is produced by staff in authentic 1890s' costume. The mill houses a coffee shop and a craft shop selling 'steam woven' goods manufactured at the mill – in particular the famous Union Shirt, a traditional garment of working men from the nineteenth century up until the mid-1950s.

Queen Street Mill to Rowley Hall

Walk back onto Queen Street, then left along the side of the mill to go left down a trackway to the gateway of Musty Haulgh Farm. Go over the stile on the right and walk on to go over fence-stile. Walk on and over to the left to go over stile in wall. Walk down and over to the right to go over fence-stile into wood. Follow the path on and down to cross the River Don by footbridge. Follow path on, over stile and

Walks from the Leeds & Liverpool Canal

on up the steps to cross the field to corner of wall. Walk on to enter the seventeenth-century farmstead of Netherwood via gate. Walk past the front of the cottages to entry gateway, then go over the stile over on the left. Walk down the narrow enclosure to go down stone steps, over stile to brook. Take the right-hand path, then over the footbridge on left. Follow path up by the side of the River Brun to enter the driveway of Rowley Hall via stile.

Netherwood displays some seventeenth-century mullioned windows on the gable, typical of a farm cottage of that time. Rowley Hall is a much grander building, having been built before 1610 by the family of Halstead of gentry/yeoman status. The house and grounds are private, so content yourself with looking at the outside from the driveway.

Rowley Hall to Towneley Hall

Walk down the drive, over bridge and on to go into trackway on the left above the play area. Follow track on, take higher track at fork to roadway at the Thornton Arms. Cross the road and walk down to go over corner stile just before the bridge. Follow the path up to the top roadway. Left, and cross the road to walk down Springwood Road, then left into Deer Park Road and on, around to the right and on down into Towneley Park. Follow the driveway on to the front of Towneley Hall.

Towneley Hall was the home of the Towneley

family from the early-fifteenth century until 1902. It is now Burnley's Art Gallery and Museum and admission is free. The Hall contains a fine collection of English oil paintings and watercolours and a large collection of Pilkington Royal Lancashire pottery, as well as some splendid Jacobean oak furniture, glassware, militaria and a local history and archaeology section. There are also period room settings, street scenes from the late-nineteenth century and displays of former local trades. The nearby Natural History Centre houses many live specimens and an aquarium. Wild flower and geological gardens have been developed outside.

Towneley Hall to Weavers' Triangle Visitor Centre

Walk down the main driveway, past Towneley High School and out onto roadway. Cross the road and walk along Parliament Street to join the canal at bridge. Follow the towpath back to the wharf.

Walks from the Leeds & Liverpool Canal 57

Walk Seven

Feniscliffe — Pleasington — Hoghton — Riley Green — Feniscowles — Feniscliffe

Distance: 7 miles, circular. Allow 5 hours with lunch.
Grade: Easy, but wear walking boots.
Lunch/Evening Meal: Butlers Arms, Pleasington/ Royal Oak, Riley Green.
Start: Witton Country Park.

DURING the 1950s, before the advent of popular motoring, this walk was a great favourite with the Blackburn mill workers. Today it is relatively quiet, but well worth exploring. The walk heads for Hoghton Tower via Pleasington Priory and returning via the canal towpath.

Witton Country Park to Pleasington Priory

From the Park Cafe follow the westerly path along the

edge of the wood, over stone footbridge and stile, then cross the field to go over stile and footbridge. Cross the playing fields to the roadway and follow it on to enter the road up to the cemetery. At the duck-pond follow the trackway to the left to enter lane. Left, and follow the lane on to the Priory and the Butler's Arms.

Pleasington Priory to Hoghton Tower

Follow the track to the right of the pub to go over stile. Over the hill, following left-hand fence, over two stiles, down to go over wall-stile. Follow right-hand wall to go over stile and on down to river bridge. Cross the bridge and walk up the lane to roadway. Right, and over stile on left to follow path up to cross the railway. Follow the path to the right to go over stile. Follow wall round, over stiles, to Hoghton Tower driveway.

Hoghton Tower to Royal Oak

After visiting the Tower, walk back down the driveway to the lodge house, turn left and go through kissing-gate. Follow left-hand fence up to go over stile. Walk down the field directly, over stile, straight down and over stile into farm lane. Walk on to Riley Green.

Riley Green to Witton Country Park

Upon leaving the inn, cross the road and follow the

Chorley/Belmont road on to join the canal towing path. Follow the towpath on, passing Feniscowles paper mills, Livesey housing estates, to leave the canal at Cherry Tree Bridge. Walk down the road to cross the main road. Right, then first left after the shops to join a pathway into Pleasington playing fields. At the end of path cross the road and follow the trackway on into Witton Park, via bridge over the River Darwen. Right and walk on to the cafe starting point.

Most likely, you have taken your lunch at the Royal Oak. This being so, may I suggest a short drive to the Butler's Arms for an evening snack or meal, children are catered for and the service and food are the finest for miles around.

Points of interest:

1. Witton Country Park has been developed from a former mill owner's country estate and holds many fine attractions. A Visitors' Centre has been developed from the Fielden Coach House and Stables: facilities include stables, harness room and coach house, with displays of harness, farm tools, horse-drawn farm machinery and several horse-drawn carriages. The Natural History Room displays the wildlife to be found on the many nature trails within the park. Also included is a lecture room and changing exhibitions are held there. Sports facilities are also numbered among the park's attractions.

60 · *Walks from the Leeds & Liverpool Canal*

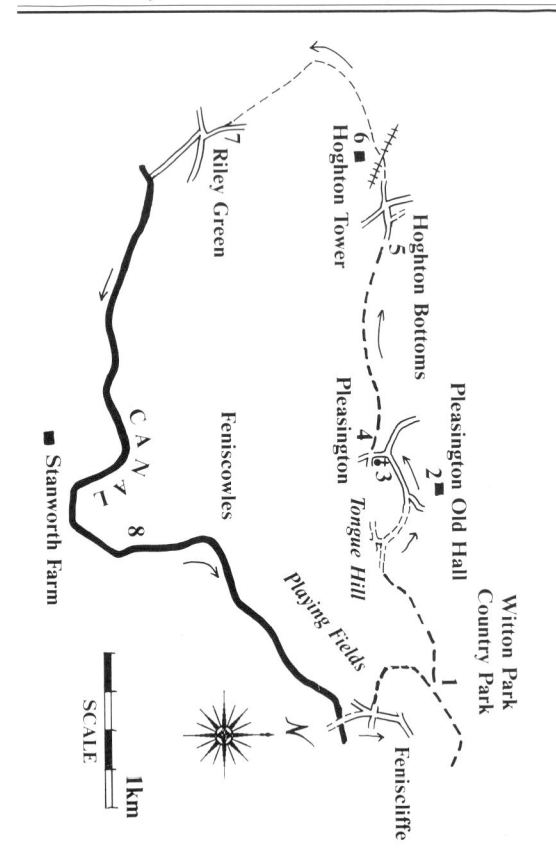

2. Pleasington Old Hall is dated 1587, and above the doorway is a carved panel bearing the arms of the Ainsworth family, with the initials of Thomas de Hoghton and John Southworth of Samlesbury, who were the chief owners of land in Pleasington. The hall stands upon the site of an earlier moated manor house and remains of the moat can still be made out in the grounds of the house. To the rear of the hall is a wildlife and butterfly garden, opened in 1987 by the botanist, David Bellamy. The hall is reputed to be the home of the 'White Lady' ghost that wanders the lanes around the Great Hall at Samlesbury. The ghost is claimed to be that of Dorothy Winckley of Pleasington Hall, who married first a Southworth, then a de Hoghton and finally Thomas Ainsworth.

3. The Roman Catholic church of St. Mary and John the Baptist, known locally as Pleasington Priory, affords a proud landmark.

   The church was built in the years 1816-19 as a thank-offering of John Francis Butler of Pleasington Hall. According to tradition, he had met with a serious accident while hunting and was very nearly killed. He resolved to erect a church there in thanks for his escape. Considering that it was built before Catholic Emancipation in 1929, it is an astonishing edifice, with its frontage modelled after that of Whalley Abbey before the Dissolution.

4. The Butler's Arms, named after the Butler family

of Pleasington Hall, is a true country inn standing amid a delightful rural landscape. The Gothic frontage blends well with the setting. The inn serves a good selection of local ales and beer and bar lunches are served from mid-day, all at very reasonable prices. A well maintained bowling green and beer garden are further attractions.

5. Thirty years ago Hoghton Bottoms was a much frequented place; tea was served by a local farmer's wife and the old mill still had its water wheel. Today, the hamlet has few visitors, the water wheel has gone and the mill stands as a relic to unwise conversion. A walk along the mill-race, through the gorge, with its towering railway arches, up as far as the weir is most rewarding. Wild garlic covers the ground and broadleafs fall to meet the river – in all, a very restful setting.

6. Hoghton Tower, a large and spectacular castellated stone mansion stands upon a spur of hill overlooking the township of Hoghton in Gunnolfsmoors – a Hiberno-Norse settlement within the Leyland Hundred. The Tower has only seen action once, leading to its fall and capture by local Parliamentarians, during February 1643.

The Hoghton family, one of Lancashire's oldest and most famous (and infamous), can trace their ancestry back to Hamon le Boteler who married a daughter of Warine Bussel, Norman Baron of Penwortham and holder of large estates in Lancashire.

The highlight of the family's history came in 1617 with the knighting of 'Sir Loin' by King James I on a visit to Sir Richard Hoghton, High Sheriff of Lancashire, known at court by the title of 'Honest Dick'. Sir Richard's son, Gilbert, also rode into the pages of history with his ill-fated 'siege' of Blackburn during the Civil War, which led to the sequestering of his estates in 1646. However, his son, another Richard, supported Cromwell and the estate was returned to the family, the decendants of whom still live on the estate today.

The Tower is open to the public: Easter Saturday, Easter Sunday, Easter Monday from 2.00 p.m. to 5 p.m; every Sunday until the end of October; Saturday, Sunday, July, August and Bank Holidays. Admission charge.

7. We would have to travel far to come across a finer wayside inn than the Royal Oak. With the inn's whitened frontage and blackened corner stones it cannot help but bring back memories of the old coaching days. Inside, beneath the low beamed ceiling, you will find many a cosy nook in which to rest, chat and enjoy good ale.

8. The canalside walk here holds great interest. As the canal enters the very western edge of industrial Blackburn, the first nineteenth-century mills begin to appear. Notice the loading and unloading facilities for the former coal barges as you pass the former mill sites.

Walk Eight

Chorley — Rivington Country Park — Anglezarke — Chorley

Distance: 8½ miles, circular.
Grade: Easy walking, but wear light boots.
Lunch: Bay Horse, Anderton or a light snack from Rivington Lower Barn.

THIS walk takes us into the Lever Park at Rivington to discover the many delights within. We return along the banks of Anglezarke Reservoir and back to the canal towpath at Chorley.

Chorley

Chorley is a small Lancashire market town. Cotton and coal formed the original economic base. The town has two markets. The covered market is open on Tuesday, Friday and Saturday, whilst the open 'Flat Iron' or cattle market is held on Tuesdays. The parish church of St. Laurence is supposed to have contained relics of the saint brought back from Normandy by Sir Rowland Standish in 1442, and the tower and parts of the chancel are from this period. The Standish and Parker pews are early- and late-seventeenth century respectively. Chorley's best known figure from the industrial revolution was the sugar manufacturer, Sir Henry Tate, who gave the nation the magnificent Tate Art Gallery in London. The best of Chorley's houses are Georgian and stand on Hollinshead Street, one having a handsome tripartite doorway with segmented fanlight.

Chorley Bus Station to canal

Walk down Union Street, left along Clifford Street, then right up Stump Lane to Eaves Lane. Right, and cross the road to walk down Froom Street to the canal towpath.

Froom Street canal bridge to Bay Horse Hotel

Follow the towpath on to leave by the second bridge after passing under the railway. Walk up the track and cross the railway. Follow lane to the right to go over stile on right of farmyard entrance. Walk on to follow left-hand fence to go over stile onto golf course. Follow yellow stakes up (around the wood) and on to follow right-hand tree-hedge to end, then walk up to club house to go over stiles on right up onto lane. Walk down the lane to go over stile

66   *Walks from the Leeds & Liverpool Canal*

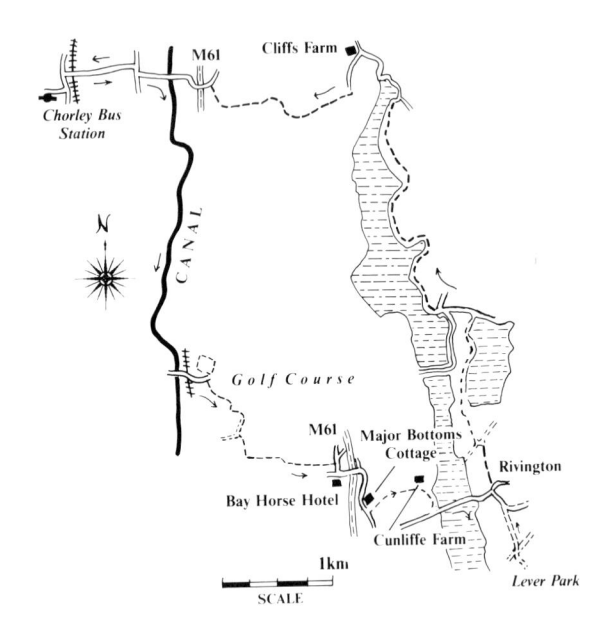

by gate at corner. Walk on to go over stile by gate on left, then follow right-hand wall on to go over stile by gate. Follow lane to the left to go over stile on right onto Stacks Farm drive. Follow drive on to go over stile by gate and on to go over next stile. Follow path on, over next stile and on up to the main road. Right, and walk on to the Bay Horse.

On to Rivington Lower Barn

Take the Rivington road, across the motorway and round to the right to go left down trackway after Major Bottoms Cottage. Follow track on, through gate and on into Cuncliffe farmyard (notice the weavers' workshop windows on ground floor). Follow farm lane down to road, left and across the reservoir. Take the lane on the right, past the old school, and on following lower path around to the Lower Barn.

Rivington Country Park

This is one of the best of Lancashire's country parks. Here one can hike or merely stroll on the numerous trails that lead one around the park or up on the high West Pennine moors. The dovecote, the ornate gardens, Rivington Pike and the replica of Liverpool Castle by the lake, are only a stride away. So are a number of sites set aside for nature conservation (we shall be walking through one soon). Lower or Great House Barn, was built in the late-sixteenth century and is constructed of large oak crucks, each side being taken from the same tree. Today it houses an information centre for visitors to the West Pennine moors, a cafe and local book shop. The adjacent stone building was once Great House Farm. This has now been converted to provide a craft shop, Ranger's office and toilets.

Lower Barn to Rivington Village

Walk down the roadside pathway, down into the village.

Rivington village

A few cottages, post office, two churches, school and village stocks – what a romantic setting to greet the eye!

The first building one notices on approaching the village from the west is the school of 1714. It was built on the site of the old free grammar school founded by Bishop Pilkington in 1566. The church across the way was built around 1540, but only a few windows remain from that period. For the most part, the church represents the rebuilding of around 1666. Inside is a monument to John Shawe, who died in 1627, in the form of a large brass plate with a skeleton on a mattress at the bottom.

Across from the village stocks stands the Unitarian Chapel of 1703. The inside is furnished with box pews and the pulpit is in the middle of the north side. By the churchyard gate can be found a collection of dated doorheads from old houses lost to the reservoir.

Rivington to Cliff's Farm

Pass through the kissing-gate opposite the chapel gates

Walks from the Leeds & Liverpool Canal

and follow the path on and down, over stile, and on to go over stile. Take the left-hand track up to lane and to follow gated metalled trackway on the right up and onto roadway via kissing-gate. Left, and walk down the road, right at the junction, on into picnic area and through kissing-gate. Follow the lane on for some way to enter nature conservation area at footpath on left. Follow path on, keeping left all the way, over stiles and onto roadway. Left, and follow road on to Cliff's Farm.

Cliff's Farm presents an interesting face to the inquiring eye. The house is dated 1696, with the initials T. A. and R. M. with a single M above. The building is a very good example of farmhouse building which can be seen in the Chorley and Heapey area.

Cliff's Farm to canal/Chorley bus station

From end of barn, follow the track up past the quarry to where paths cross. Walk up the right-hand path to go over stiles and on up to cairn. Take the left-hand path on down, across other path, and on down to go over stile. Follow path down, and along the edge of field to go over stile. Follow path on to the right to go over stile onto mill driveway. Left and on over the motorway and canal bridges to walk up Froom Street. Cross Eaves Lane and walk down Stump Lane, on over the railway to go left along Clifton Street. Turn right into Union Street and walk on to the bus station.

Walk Nine

Wigan Pier — Haigh Hall Country Park — Wigan

Distance: 8 miles, return.
Grade: Very easy; walking shoes.
Lunch: Kirkless Hall Inn, Top Lock.

FROM the major heritage development of Wigan Pier up through the impressive Wigan flight of 21 locks to the wild and romantic Haigh Hall Country Park, this walk passes through some fascinating landscapes and shows the visitor the best that Wigan has to offer and the contrasting aspects of Wigan Borough. A return can be made from the country park by local bus, allowing one a greater freedom of time to discover what is on offer.

Wigan Pier

The name Wigan Pier was first coined as a joke by the music hall star George Formby Senior at the

Walks from the Leeds & Liverpool Canal

expense of the seaside resorts of Southport and Blackpool. Later, George Orwell, in his book *The Road to Wigan Pier*, in his search for this wonder, used it as a symbol of decay for the falling fortunes of the industrial North.

Today the 'pier' stands at the heart of a unique complex of canalside warehouses and mill buildings. Concerts and conferences are housed at 'The Mill at the Pier'. In the 'Schools Centre' and on floating classrooms, guided by resident tutors, children study their heritage. The Pier boasts the largest working steam engine in the world, the Trencherfield Engine, and the 'Way We Were' Heritage Centre, with exhibitions of local life in the late-nineteenth and early-twentieth centuries.

Wigan Pier is open from 10 a.m. to 5 p.m. every day except Christmas Day and Boxing Day. General enquiries (0942) 323666.

Wigan Pier to Top Lock

Join the canal towpath at the rear of the Wigan Pier Information Centre and follow it all the way up to the Kirkless Hall Inn at Top Lock.

Kirkless Hall

Kirkless Hall stands in a field to the left of the towpath just before Top Lock. The building is of brick with a mock-timber framed entrance porch. A datestone to the left of the porch records a date of 1663, but I doubt that this refers to the exterior.

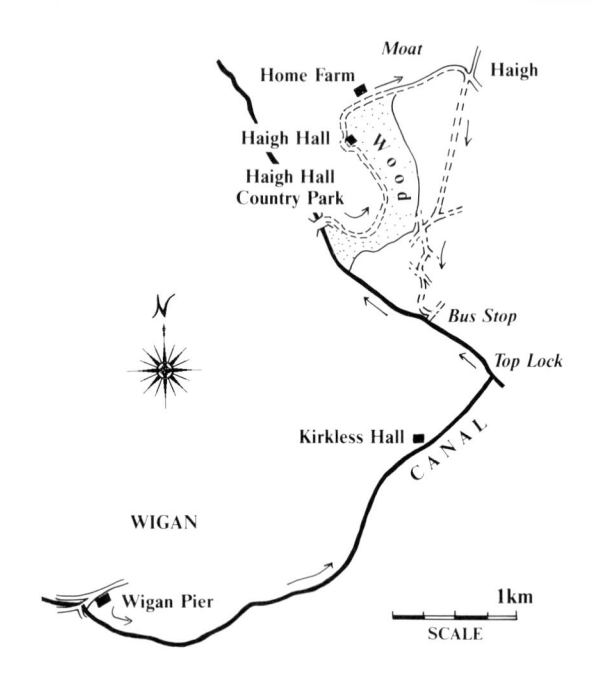

The inn looks out onto the canal locks, and on a fine day tables are placed outside so that folk can enjoy the view of water traffic. The food and beer

Walks from the Leeds & Liverpool Canal

served are to a very high standard, and very reasonably priced too.

Top Lock to Haigh Country Park

Follow the towpath on to leave by the third bridge after Top Lock, situated in the wooded section. Walk up the drive to Haigh Hall and on to Stables Visitors.

Anciently, Haigh Hall, of which place only the moat still survives, was the home of the Earls of Crawford and Balcarres.

A curious tale is handed down through history referring to the hall's residents in the early 1300s: Sir William Bradshaigh and his wife, Lady Mabel, were dwelling at the hall when in 1315 Sir Adam de Banastre of Shevington and Charnock Richard called upon Sir William to rise up against Thomas, Earl of Lancaster. Along with other local landowners, they set forth. The two forces clashed at Deepdale, near Preston, and the Banastre Rebellion was crushed. Sir Adam and others were executed, but Sir William fled into exile and was later presumed dead. After this time Lady Mabel remarried, but after the death of Thomas, Earl of Lancaster, Sir William returned and slew the usurper. Mabel was reunited with her former husband, and by way of penance her confessor bade her to walk 'onest every week barefoot and bare-legged to a cross near Wigan from the Haghe'. The cross stands in Standishgate and is known today as

Mab's Cross.

The last of the Bradshaighs died in 1770 and the estate passed to Alexander Lindsay, 23rd Earl of Crawford. He started an ironwork foundry building colliery machinery, as well as investing heavily in the Leeds and Liverpool Canal.

Today, Haigh Park provides plenty to attract visitors. There are woodland walks and nature trails, a small zoo with a variety of exotic animals and an eighteen-hole golf course. For the children, there are model and miniature railways, a model village, playground and picnic areas. The Stables Centre includes a cafe and offers a good starting point for exploration.

On to Wigan (via canal or bus)

Coming out through the Stables Centre archway, follow the drive round to the right and walk down the main drive to Haigh village. Turn left into the trackway opposite the pub and follow it on to enter pathway. Follow the path down to trackway, go right and walk on to go left at roadway, over the bridge and on down to go into signed footpath on right. Walk down to go over footbridge. Follow path up to trackway, left, and walk on to roadway. Turn right, and on down to the canal to return to Wigan Pier, or you may catch the bus from here to the town centre – a five-minute ride.

Wigan

Wigan first came to light as the Roman town of Coccium, built upon the summit of the elevation in the centre of the town, on which the parish church of All Saints now stands. Sadly, little remains to be seen today, but inside the church there is the head of a Roman altar. At nearby Dalton a headless statue of Cautopates, one of the attendants of the god Mithras, was found, possibly indicating the site of the Mithraic Temple. This now stands in the Ribchester Museum. Meaningless away from its true context, it should be returned to where it was found, in Dalton.

During the post-Roman, Celtic period, Wigan was the capital of Greater Makerfield, later re-formed into the 'hundreds' of the northern Lancashire plain.

Today, Wigan is undoubtedly one of the finest towns in Lancashire. The old city centre street pattern has been maintained, offering a selection of shops and inns hard to find anywhere north of Chester or Manchester. All in all, well worth a visit.

Walk Ten

Rufford — Croston — Rufford

Distance: 7 miles circular.
Grade: Very easy walking; light boots.
Lunch: Croston: Lord Nelson, Wheatsheaf or Crown Inn on Station Road.

HERE we follow rivers, a canal and field ditches through the crop growing lands of the Lancashire plain. All manner of vegetables grow in the rich soils of Croston Moss, and in the villages of Rufford and Croston the agrarian tradition in village life lives on. Truly a glimpse back to a former age of rural life.

Rufford Old Hall

Rufford Old Hall, built by the Heskeths in the late-fifteenth century, with seventeenth-century additions, is a very picturesque half-timbered house. The interior of the house is overpowering, with an exuberance of decoration matched nowhere else in the county – the

Walks from the Leeds & Liverpool Canal

Map showing:
- old course R. Douglas
- R. Lostock
- Croston
- Croston Parish Church
- CANAL (Rufford Branch)
- R. Douglas
- Sumner's Farm
- Rufford Old Hall
- The Sluice
- RUFFORD
- 1km SCALE
- N

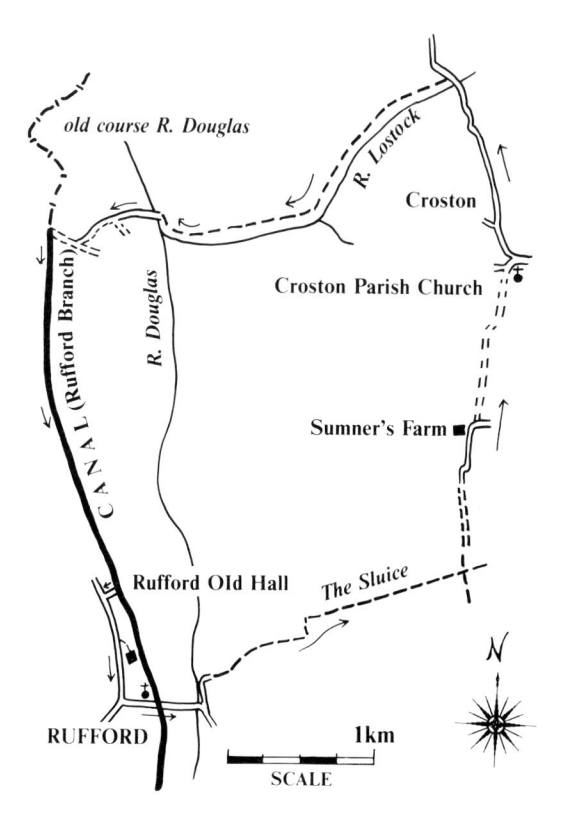

decorated hammer-beams, the great monster of a screen with its barbaric shapes are only two of the impressive features that compete for the eye.

You can view the hall, with its collections of sixteenth-century arms and armour, oak furniture and period costumes from 24th March to 5th November, every day except Friday, 1 p.m. to 5 p.m., Sunday 2 p.m. to 5 p.m. Admission charge.

Rufford Old Hall to Croston Church

Leave the Hall grounds and follow the main road to the left, to go left again down the Parbold road, past the Parish Church of St. Mary, over the canal and railway bridges to turn into track on left after road bridge. Follow the track on, over flat bridge then right to follow sluice up to go left at corner and directly on to ditch boundary. Right, and follow ditch boundary on, across field road, and on, through hedgerow and on to field lane. Left, and follow the field lane on up, past Summer's Farm and on along the lane into Croston. Cross the stone footbridge, right and down Church Street into the churchyard.

The approach to the church is flanked by terraces of brick cottages of around 1704, the entrance of which is home to the village cross, mounted upon steps. It is from the cross that we first notice the slanted church tower (most of the buildings in Croston are leaning this way due to the marshy nature of the ground).

The church itself is late-Gothic, with strange

additions and rebuilding work done between 1577 and 1823. Worthy of note inside the church are a thirteenth-century double piscina, a fifteenth-century aumbry and a font of 1663.

The village displays many periods of cottage architecture, all leaning one way or the other, that date from the sixteenth century onwards. The almshouses, a long, low building on Station Road, has a datestone of 1692 that informs us that they were endowed by Henry and Isabel Croston at that time. Near the church we find the Yarrow Bridge which is dated 1682, and nearby the Rectory gateway, a tripartite Gothic piece with ogee arches, which is apparently meant to appear ruinous. The classic view of the village is one looking down Church Street with the cross in the foreground.

Croston to Rufford

From the parish church, walk up Church Street, left and follow Town Road through the village and on into Station Road (the almshouses are over on the right). Follow road on, over railway bridge and on to go over stile on the left after crossing Lostock Bridge. Follow the riverside path on to cross Red Bridge. Follow the lane on to the canal towpath. Left, and follow the towpath on to leave by the third bridge. Walk on to the main road, left and on to Rufford Old Hall.